THE DARK SIDE OF ASIAN WOMEN

WHAT TO EXPECT FROM AN ASIAN WOMAN BEFORE IT HAPPENS

THE DARK SIDE OF ASIAN WOMEN

DANIEL MARQUES

THE DARK SIDE OF

ASIAN WOMEN

WHAT TO EXPECT FROM AN ASIAN WOMAN
BEFORE IT HAPPENS

DANIEL MARQUES

THE DARK SIDE OF ASIAN WOMEN

DANIEL MARQUES

Copyright © Daniel Marques, 2012

Cover Photo © davetada Via Flickr

No part of this book may be reproduced in any form,

or by any means, without permission from the author.

THE DARK SIDE OF ASIAN WOMEN

DANIEL MARQUES

CONTENTS

INTRODUCTION

SEX

MARRIAGE

SUICIDE

REVENGE

MANIPULATION

SECRETS

MONEY

BIOGRAPHY

ABOUT THE BOOK

BOOKS FROM THE AUTHOR

THE DARK SIDE OF ASIAN WOMEN

INTRODUCTION

THE DARK SIDE OF ASIAN WOMEN

INTRODUCTION

Asian women are among men's most favorite, due to their caring behavior, dedication to family values and, obviously, for being among the most beautiful women in the world.

Nonetheless, they have a dark side, not known to many.

This book resumes years of interviews to women in Asia, regarding their expectations, believes and behaviors before and after marriage, but also interviews with men that married them.

This is a book that reveals a dark tendency that has crossed the centuries and is very well present nowadays, not only among women in Asia but also the ones that went abroad.

Not forgetting the fact that these tendencies tend to change with women that live outside Asia for many years, it's mostly directed to uncover the strongest presence of the evil acts in Asian countries.

It has been compared, for the purpose of this book, both the younger and older generations of women, but also the ones that have no contact with foreigners in their country, those that do but never went abroad, and finally those that have actually been abroad, the ones that had or didn't had relationships with foreigners, and how they all think and feel about their own experiences.

DANIEL MARQUES

In this short manual it's possible to find a resume to hundreds of pages of collected information and face-to-face interviews.

Probably, an Asian woman could write a much more accurate manual, with all the dirty tricks they know and share among themselves every time they meet; however, this is a book written by a man based on his direct observation, investigation and conclusions.

Even though not trying to discriminate Asian women in any way, this book intends to clarify most of their behaviors, often originated in a still very immature and damaged culture.

May the knowledge here presented help in the fulfillment of better and more loving relationships, not only for men that date and marry Asian women, but also for these women, in the exact same level, because the only way to stop something negative from persisting consists in exposing it.

It's not what this book can do for men, but what men can do with what this book provides.

The dark side of Asian women is in fact a heritage that often condemns them to bitterness and a life without love.

In bringing light into the darkness may we all be more enlightened about the truth and the meaning of love in relationships.

THE DARK SIDE OF ASIAN WOMEN

SEX

THE DARK SIDE OF ASIAN WOMEN

SEX

One of the most common situations is when she requests to have sex without condom.

Whatever she may say, it means that she wants a baby from you or a baby and you, or just you but the baby is the only available solution for that purpose.

Asian women fear being abandoned by men and tend to be immature when dealing with relationships, but they also tend to fear getting old and lose their attraction; and they are at the same time very much attached to their lover and so often that the only possible solution they usual find to keep a man is by having his baby.

Is she loves a man to the point of wishing his baby it's possible to rethink about the relationship and plan for the future. But, there's no need to leave a woman in such condition.

Doing that would be very traumatic to the woman, as the only reason she does this is related to love and fear of losing that same love.

The best behavior consists in making her understand your true plans in life.

If she loves you she will understand and wait. But "wait" is here the right word, as almost all Asian women, soon or later, do want children in their relationships.

It's a very strong topic within Asian Cultures.

Some women, either very young, or already in their 40s, want a baby so much that they will have sex without protection with as many men as possible until they have what they want.

For some, and at a certain point in their life, having a baby becomes more important than having a man.

THE DARK SIDE OF ASIAN WOMEN

MARRIAGE

THE DARK SIDE OF ASIAN WOMEN

MARRIAGE

Marriage in itself is not a negative thing, but wanting it before even knowing the other person, yes.

Many Asian women have daily fantasies about meeting a foreigner man and marrying him, have a family with him, etc.

The dreams can go so far in their imagination that very often, when meeting one for the first or second time, they already have the whole story programmed in their head – what to do with you, how, in which manner, etc.

It's important to acknowledge their fantasies in order to avoid hurting them.

Asian women are very sensitive and into American romantic movies, which are totally out of the Asian reality and very often just do more harm than good.

The best solution in dealing with these situations consists in gradually teaching them about the personality of the man they're dealing with and slowly bring them to reality without confronting in a way that may make them burst into tears of disappointment; something like…

"We haven't kissed enough to talk about marriage, I think! What do you think?"

Or,

"You know, in the movies, everything happens very fast because it has one hour and a half, but you can't rush life in one hour and a half and compress it all there. Don't you agree?"

Their immaturity about life and relationships is what makes them special and at the same a headache for the less patient men.

Many take advantage of this to fuck as much as they want, but I would say that such behavior is pure evil and very disrespectful.

You can still fuck as many women as you want while being honest with them.

In fact, in the beginning, if you don't feed their dreams, they will very likely still be willing to have just sex for personal pride.

Even though they all have the expectation of something more, many, especially the young ones, want mostly the experience of having sex with different men and they see this as something to be proud about, even though always hiding it from society.

If you don't hurt them and you don't make false promises, you can have a pretty relaxing life with many girls at the same time, which will know about your affairs and still allow it.

This reality is very common in China and Japan, where men tend to have multiple affairs after marriage.

Even though the rate of divorce is Asia is as high as in any other country around the world, here, to divorce is something to be shamed about and highly avoided. So, knowing that their husband is having sex with other women is never a topic of conversation or motive for divorce.

Is Asian countries, it's more common for men to ask for divorce than the opposite.

DANIEL MARQUES

SUICIDE

THE DARK SIDE OF ASIAN WOMEN

SUICIDE

If an Asian woman is deeply in love she may kill herself if abandoned by her lover.

She will tell you and she may really do it.

Asian women don't have enough experience in dealing with emotions and, as Asia keeps developing into a more modern society, the contrast of the old traditions with the new behaviors seen in movies is too big.

On one hand they're more open minded about love, relationships and sex, but on the other hand they don't have enough skills to deal with all the events that may occur.

They suffer more as the number of failed relationships increases and often take on themselves all the guilt and depreciation about themselves.

These women tend to believe that if a man leaves them is because they are not beautiful enough, rich enough or nice enough; and they'll carry this burden and accumulate even more each time they fail.

This means that an Asian woman with many failed relationships tends to have more difficulties to be who she is and love a man.

The fear of suffering, of having to start all over again, searching for a new boyfriend, can be so devastating that she will drop on the floor in tears and grab you strongly, beginning for you not to leave her during a breakup.

If you do, she'll tell you that her life has no purpose and she'll kill herself if you don't come back.

The reason why japan has such a high percentage of suicides resides, in many cases, in the fact that single Japanese women feel ashamed of their status and commit suicide.

Nevertheless, while some actually try and do it, many just think about it, while others look at death in the face, from their very high 30 floors buildings, and rethink about the whole thing.

Even so, they usually take months to recover from a breakup, and many still suffer after starting a new relationship or after their ex is long gone to a faraway country, and very often in both situations; meaning they have difficulties to restart new relationships and forget previous ones at the same time.

It's because they suffer so much with their emotions that they often keep distant relationships.

This is also something historical in Asian countries, as the man of the family, in ancient times, would leave the wife to go find work in a distant land, and then he would send her money and letters at distance.

THE DARK SIDE OF ASIAN WOMEN

Asian people love this kind of impossible and unfulfilled love as well as movies that portray it, and that's why many of their romantic movies and stories end up in tragedy.

They love the "unhappy ending" in which the lover dies in battle or they both commit suicide to stay together in the afterlife.

Many will not marry the one they love, because they also believe an impossible love is much more pure and romantic.

Romeo and Juliet story is very popular in Asia because of its very Asian in style.

Unfortunately, there isn't a proper solution for this reality or any significant changes in later times, because while Asian men often abandon their women no matter what they say, without any demonstration of compassion (and compassion is definitely not one of the qualities in Asian people), Psychologists, from west to east, still don't present efective solutions for suicide.

From a personal perspective, I would say that when such threat occurs it's better not to abandon the woman, while also not making her realize that she won something.

It's very much like educating an immature child, because these reactions arise due to lack of experience in dealing with emotions, immaturity, even though the situation here is much more serious.

Nevertheless, it's important, in the following days to this event, to make her slowly realize that the relationship has no future, while creating more distance between both until she feels comfortable with and accepts the breakup with a clear mind.

The safer solution always consists in educating her in dealing with the emotions, while slowly preparing her to the end of that relationship.

On the other hand, as adult education is not as easy as child education, the most likely behavior to expect, when she does accept the breakup, is some kind of hatred revenge to clean her image.

Among the most likely to happen, are the "having sex with another man", "start dating another person" and "steal personal objects or money".

It's important to notice, however, that Asian men do exactly the same.

THE DARK SIDE OF ASIAN WOMEN

DANIEL MARQUES

REVENGE

THE DARK SIDE OF ASIAN WOMEN

REVENGE

Revenge is a very serious subject in the Asian culture.

It can take as long as needed, as far as it takes, but no Asian forgets it.

Asians may even have to live with what you did, but they'll never forget it, and if the opportunity comes, no matter how many years have passed, they will make you pay.

A Chinese woman, even though not having the tendency to be aggressive, in anger and for revengeful purposes, can go as far as to killing a man.

The killing in the Asian culture, though, is very different from the American way or what we may be used to see in movies.

Asians don't like confrontation or demonstrations of violence; they also don't like to lose in their attempts; so, here, the most common aggression is poisoning.

This strategy is as ancient as modern, and goes from the Communist Government of China and its spies until the most common of citizens.

If you do something to someone in China, for example, and then go to a surrounding restaurant or coffee shop, and after eating or drinking a coffee you feel very sick, with diarrhea and vomiting, feel happy for having your body detecting it and getting rid of it on the spot.

The worse that can happen is the body not having any reaction.

Even though food intoxication is a common thing, in Asia, poisoning is as much, leaving many in the doubt if they survived a poisoning attempt or a rotten fish.

It is however relatively easy to see the difference.

When you are poisoned, you actually feel like you're going to die; you'll feel pain in the stomach, loss of conscience, etc.

Other abnormal factors may help indicate food poisoning, like an extremely sweet Coffee, as it's much more common for the coffee to be bitter with no sugar at all.

Luckily, unless you are dealing with governmental issues, the majority of the population is not very effective in doing this, and will very likely "just" poison you with some rat poison or something else similar to it.

Asians don't like to lose face so, while smiling to you, eyes to eyes, they will very likely send someone else that you never saw before to do the dirty work.

In the Asian culture, this action is nearly religious, as everyone will act together for the final purpose.

THE DARK SIDE OF ASIAN WOMEN

Asians are self-protective, nationalistic, proud and very often racist; if you're a foreigner that cheated, attacked, raped or abandoned an Asian woman, even the waiter in a restaurant will help in the killing.

To understand this issue better, know that there're reported stories in newspapers concerning Foreigners being beaten by mobs after fighting with hookers.

If a hooker slaps your face after you refuse her nobody reacts, but if you slap her back more than 10 security guards will jump on you.

Moreover, in countries like China, not only the Police will not interfere, the government will use these situations to promote propaganda against foreigners and at the same time as a tool to stimulate nationalistic unity against a common enemy.

In Singapore, where the prostitutes are among the most gorgeous in Asia but also tend to be under age, rape is convicted with life sentence.

When you're dealing with governmental issues, and God may prohibit you from having sex or even a blowjob with any daughter of politicians from China or Korea, you're nowhere safe, from the hotel to the airport.

It's well known in the Asian culture that a lie can save many lies; so, if you feel danger, lie about where you are going, where you are staying and when you're coming back, even if you never will.

This is how men escape in Asia; they pure and simply disappear; and even though later on they end up accused of being spies, again to promote hatred feelings against foreigners, more than often they're not.

Asians are ridiculously paranoid when they want to attack a person, specially a foreigner, even without any proves whatsoever.

As a matter of fact, in many Asian countries such as China, a word of a local against a foreigner is much more valuable than any proves he may have.

Some foreigners have been accused of being spies just because they enjoyed taking pictures, even though those pictures prove absolutely nothing, while others have had people entering their apartments to leave something to later accuse them with.

Drugs in China means dead penalty with a shot in the head, while, ironically you'll see it being sold in many places where corrupted cops can also be found.

A person that has open access to your house, like a girlfriend, can easily buy a certain amount and place it there before saying…

THE DARK SIDE OF ASIAN WOMEN

"Ok! I accept that our relationship is over!"

MANIPULATION

THE DARK SIDE OF ASIAN WOMEN

MANIPULATION

For Asian women, love isn't as important as a solid relationship, therefore, they have many strategies to keep a man, no matter what he feels or doesn't about them.

Most of those strategies consist in spying on his mobile to know what he does and who he meets, as well as keeping a record of everything there, but also spying on the computer, get passwords to access the email and other accounts and, more commonly, leaving objects in the man's house so that they can come back to "pick them up".

Some women may even give him a credit card to access a second bank account in order to lead him to think that he has access to their money.

Others will take every opportunity they can to take their man to travel, in which the main purpose is to disconnect him from female rivals and friends that could advise to leave her.

Knowing your friends is also very important for them as a way to better understand what you think and your values.

Basically speaking, knowing where you are all the time, during work or outside work, and having things with you that belong to them, or holding on to things belonging to you, is their most effective strategy to make sure you'll never runaway.

The possible solution here would be to mislead them as they never give up on finding these things, and make them believe they have all they need.

On the other hand, if they already know too much about you, then you have to, like in war times, just go away and leave everything behind.

Asian men are more smart in dealing with such things, or maybe more cruel, as they often plan everything ahead, while making love to their woman and smiling in her face; they then leave unseen with all their stuff and, sometimes, also with the woman's money.

THE DARK SIDE OF ASIAN WOMEN

SECRETS

THE DARK SIDE OF ASIAN WOMEN

SECRETS

While there's a beautiful Asia that looks very naïve, mysterious and peaceful, there's a second one that is very perverse and immoral.

You may not be able to easily kiss an Asian woman on the street or even flirt with her, but you can easily bring a strange woman home and once there have the wildest sex with her.

The same applies for orgies; while Asians appear to be very pudic regarding sex, the fact is that orgies and prostitution are very common in Asian; basically, if with close doors and in total privacy, everything is possible.

That may well explain also the fact that they have the largest population on earth.

It's something like "if you don't tell, they won't tell" and, if only you two know, then there isn't any limitation to what can happen, even if she already has a boyfriend or husband.

In fact, when an Asian woman goes to a man's house she already knows the purpose and if she plays hard to get this is just part of the whole game, a game in which they want to see what you are willing to do to go to the end of it.

Don't be surprised, for the same reason, if she refuses to go home with you in front of her friends.

The "losing face" concept is very important in Asia; everything must be done in total secrecy.

This is so true that while Pornography is banned in China, this is also the country with the biggest population in the world and highest number of cheating husbands and spouses.

At the same time, in Asian countries such as the Philippines, Japanese and Korean women are known for travelling there for sex, especially if they're married.

Asian countries, especially China and Thailand, are also popular for having the highest rate of prostitutes per habitant and, more surprisingly, many will do it for extra money, as a part-time job, or for fun, more than an actual need or due to lack of options in life.

Many young girls in China prostitute themselves to buy a Smartphone or iPad, but also to travel to other countries and pay for College, or merely because they didn't want an average daily job from morning to evening.

Interestingly, and as surprising as it may seem for many western men, Asians do enjoy sex very much, just like they enjoy food and sleeping.

It's a basic-needs-based culture; the more sleeping, eating and fucking they have the happier they are.

Nonetheless, without wishing to stereotype Asians, we must be aware that this is only the tendency and not an exception or rule.

According to Female standards in Asia, the perfect Asian woman will sleep no less than eight hours a day, eat like a pig, look as slim as a model, be sexier than a hooker and fuck more variety of men than French women wish to.

If what is written here was not true, they would not end up so often robbed in Italy and Spain by men that seduce them for casual sex; and, after being married, as well as far beyond their 40s, would not use shorter skirts and bigger high heels than Polish hookers.

This however is not discrimination, firstly because this book is only dedicated to explain the Darkside of Asian women in general, and not men, which in fact is much darker than the one in women, and secondly because we may notice that Amsterdam, in the country were Prostitution and Drugs have been legalized, is the favorite destination of Asian Married men, especially officials of the Government.

Don't forget however that literally everything in this chapter…

It's A SECRET!!! SHHHHH!!!!

A secret, I must say, that their companions, waiting at home while they travel on "business trips" don't want to know about.

For almost all Asians, men and women, the lie is better than the painful truth.

They call it "white lie" as many witches in Europe would call themselves white sorcerers.

I wonder myself if there's such thing as a white lie, or even "white crime", "white sex", "white drug" and white "immorality"???

Nevertheless, this book intends to show the darkest of truths in Asia and not the "whiter" of them or propose its understanding.

THE DARK SIDE OF ASIAN WOMEN

DANIEL MARQUES

MONEY

THE DARK SIDE OF ASIAN WOMEN

MONEY

Last but not least, it's important to know that the Asian culture is money driven.

Maybe due to many decades of war and poverty in the last century, the fact is that Asian women have adopted a particular attitude regarding money that often means they will try to marry the richest man they can find, no matter what they may or not feel for such man.

It's not uncommon to see a gorgeous Asian woman next to an old and fat, as well as ugly, man with an Audi, Porsche or Ferrari.

The tendency for such behavior goes more far than this, as they tend to date many men at the same time, and measure which one to choose by allowing them to pay for things – dinners, gifts, travels, etc.

They will always choose the one that spends more money on them.

Even though this book is dedicated to explore the darkest side in women, men also do this, and they often abandon their wife, even in modern times, to marry a richer one.

Even though not many Asians can accept or tolerate it, the right thing to do regards setting principles from the very beginning and avoid paying for anything.

It's a fact as well that many beautiful, independent and really nice women can understand this.

However, they tend to be the exception.

It's relatively simple to test what kind of woman you're dating if you say, when meeting the girl in a coffee shop:

"Do you want to drink something?"

In very rare cases, she will get up to pick the drink herself, while the vast majority will ask you to do it yourself.

Paying for drinks is not as serious as the tendency that this implies, as women expect also to be the holders of the man's credit card after marriage.

They will do everything they can to have it, and when they do, they basically accept everything else.

Many women spend weekends alone sleeping with only a credit card, reason why they refuse to divorce in the most obvious of the situations.

THE DARK SIDE OF ASIAN WOMEN

It's all as pathetic as it is sad.

Their extremely dependency on men condemns them to a lonely fate of illusions and lies.

In some cases, which include recently married young couples, sometimes of Foreigner men with Chinese women, the woman refuses to divorce even if not having sex for more than a year with her husband, including when they sleep in separate rooms.

There're also many cases of gay men that marry to continue being accepted by their family and women that, while knowing this before marriage, accept it gladly, especially if he's rich.

In some cases, these men have sons but don't visit their wives more than one month every year for more than 20 years.

This to say that marriage for an Asian woman means everything, even though it may be absolutely nothing.

BIOGRAPHY

THE DARK SIDE OF ASIAN WOMEN

BIOGRAPHY

Daniel Marques is the Author of more than 20 Amazon Bestsellers, including "Alpha Power", "Rules of Seduction" and "Ultimate Sex Manual", and has written more than 71 books about Spirituality, Conscience, Wisdom and Sexuality. His background experience includes working as a Professor for 4 Universities in subjects related to Business, Human Resources Management, Entrepreneurship, E-Commerce, Academic Writing & Research, Foreign Language & Culture, as well as Teaching Methodologies, but also Business Consultant, Director of Multinational Training Companies, Principal of a Private University, Psychopedagogist (Expert in Learning Disabilities), Translator, Designer (award-winner), Primary School Teacher and High School Teacher for Psychology, Sociology, Philosophy, Mathematics, Science, History, Sports and Language. In the Spiritual field, he was an active member of many different Religious Societies, Sects & Cults, working closely with their top and older members & having access to the most secret knowledge kept in books and shared in close-door meetings, but has also worked as a Fortune-teller & Spiritual Adviser.

DANIEL MARQUES

ABOUT THE BOOK

THE DARK SIDE OF ASIAN WOMEN

ABOUT THE BOOK

Asian women are among men's most favorite, due to their caring behavior, dedication to family values and, obviously, for being among the most beautiful women in the world. Nonetheless, they have a dark side, not known to many. This book resumes years of interviews to women in Asia, regarding their expectations, believes and behaviors before and after marriage, but also interviews with men that married them. This is a book that reveals a dark tendency that has crossed the centuries and is very well present nowadays, not only among women in Asia but also the ones that went abroad. Not forgetting the fact that these tendencies tend to change with women that live outside Asia for many years, it's mostly directed to uncover the strongest presence of the evil acts in Asian countries. It has been compared, for the purpose of this book, both the younger and older generations of women, but also the ones that have no contact with foreigners in their country, those that do but never went abroad, and finally those that have actually been abroad, the ones that had or didn't had relationships with foreigners, and how they all think and feel about their own experiences. In this short manual it's possible to find a resume to hundreds of pages of collected information and face-to-face interviews. May the knowledge here presented help in the fulfillment of better and more loving relationships, not only for men that date and marry Asian women, but also for these women, in the exact same level, because the only way to stop something negative from persisting consists in exposing it. The dark side of Asian women is in fact a heritage that often condemns them to bitterness and a life without love. In bringing light into the darkness may we all be more enlightened about the truth and the meaning of love in relationships.

THE DARK SIDE OF ASIAN WOMEN

BOOKS
FROM THE AUTHOR

BOOKS FROM THE AUTHOR

41 Books in English

- The Dark Side of Asian Women
- Dating Asian Women
- How to Sexually Arouse Women (4 Books)
- Alpha Power
- The rules of seduction
- The Ultimate Sex Manual (For Men/Women)
- Creative Souls
- Feel and Grow Rich
- What is "The Secret"?
- Implants
- New World Order
- What We Want & Why We're Coming Back
- Prophets and Prophecies

- Asian Secrets and Tips for Weight Loss
- Immortal
- Spiritual DNA
- The 111 Most Hidden Secret Laws
- The 88 Secret Codes of the Power Elite
- The Spiritual Laws of Money
- The Greatest Power
- The secrets behind "the secret"
- 2012, China & Beyond
- Born to Be Alive!
- Kill Your God!
- Creative Lovers
- Alpha Female
- Apocalypse
- Danmar Kung Fu
- Penis on a Leash
- Why you should listen to me
- Why you should Believe in Me

THE DARK SIDE OF ASIAN WOMEN

- The Path to Success
- Heart to Heart
- Heart on Fire
- Fairy Tales from Ancient times
- How to Write & Publish your own Book
- For Lazy Teachers Only

DANIEL MARQUES

30 Books in Portuguese

- Ego Sentio, Ergo Sum
- Sabedoria Espiritual
- Amor (Vol. 1, 2 e 3)
- A China Não Existe
- A Lei de Deus
- Positivamente
- Energia Vital
- A Ciência da Alma
- Autoterapia Psicológica
- Karma
- A Metodologia Pedagógica
- A Verdade
- Dualidades Existências
- Recrutamento e Selecção
- Demónios
- Diabólica

THE DARK SIDE OF ASIAN WOMEN

- Técnicas de Estudo para Crianças
- Porquê que as Pessoas Boas Sofrem?
- O Caminho para a Consciência
- O Caminho da Sabedoria
- O melhor estudante
- O estudante eficiente
- Quinze Residências num Ano
- As Saudades que te Oculto
- Insanidade Complementar
- Ser Feliz
- Fábulas da Floresta
- Inexistir

WEBSITES

THE DARK SIDE OF ASIAN WOMEN

WEBSITES

BOOKS: www.amazon.com/author/danmarques

BLOG: www.danielmarques.tk
or danmarquesbooks.wordpress.com

Twitter: twitter.com/danmarquesbooks

To book Daniel for a Speaking Engagement, or Coaching Services (Live and at Distance), contact by email at **danmarquesbooks@gmail.com.**

If you have enjoyed reading this book kindly leave your review on…

www.amazon.com/author/danmarques

Printed in Great Britain
by Amazon.co.uk, Ltd.,
Marston Gate.